I0479672

THIS JOURNAL BELONGS TO

____

____

____

Imprint: Independently published

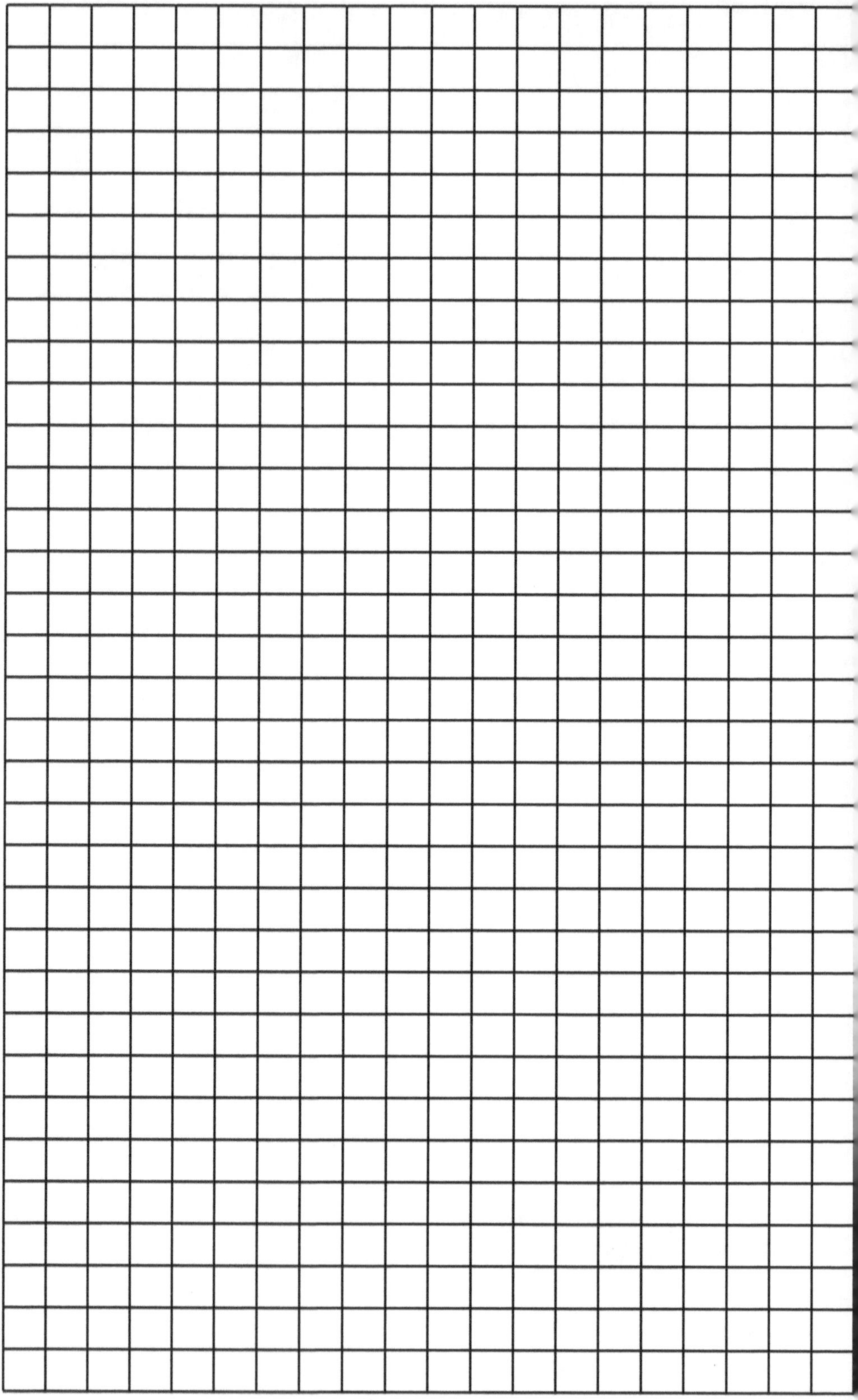

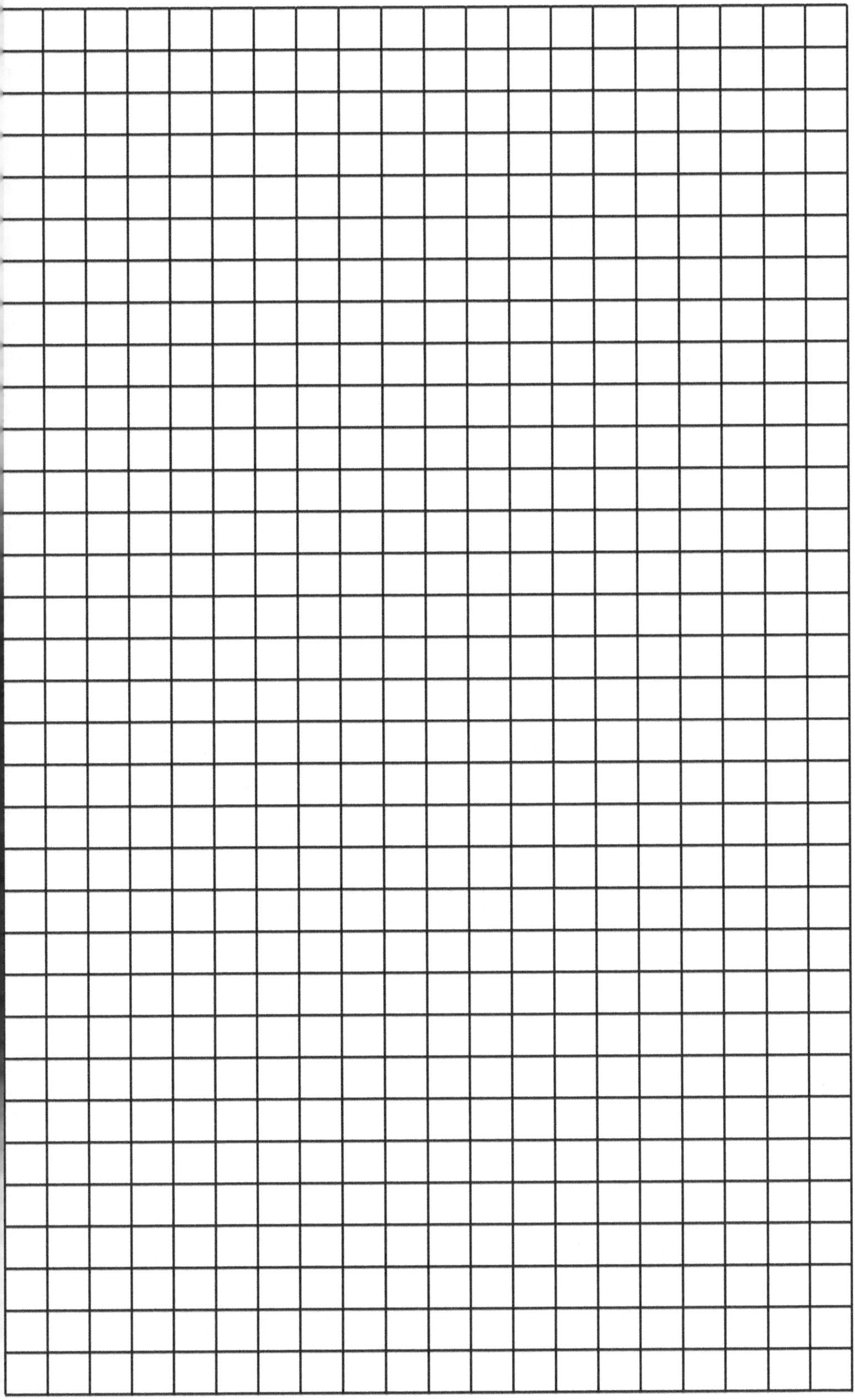

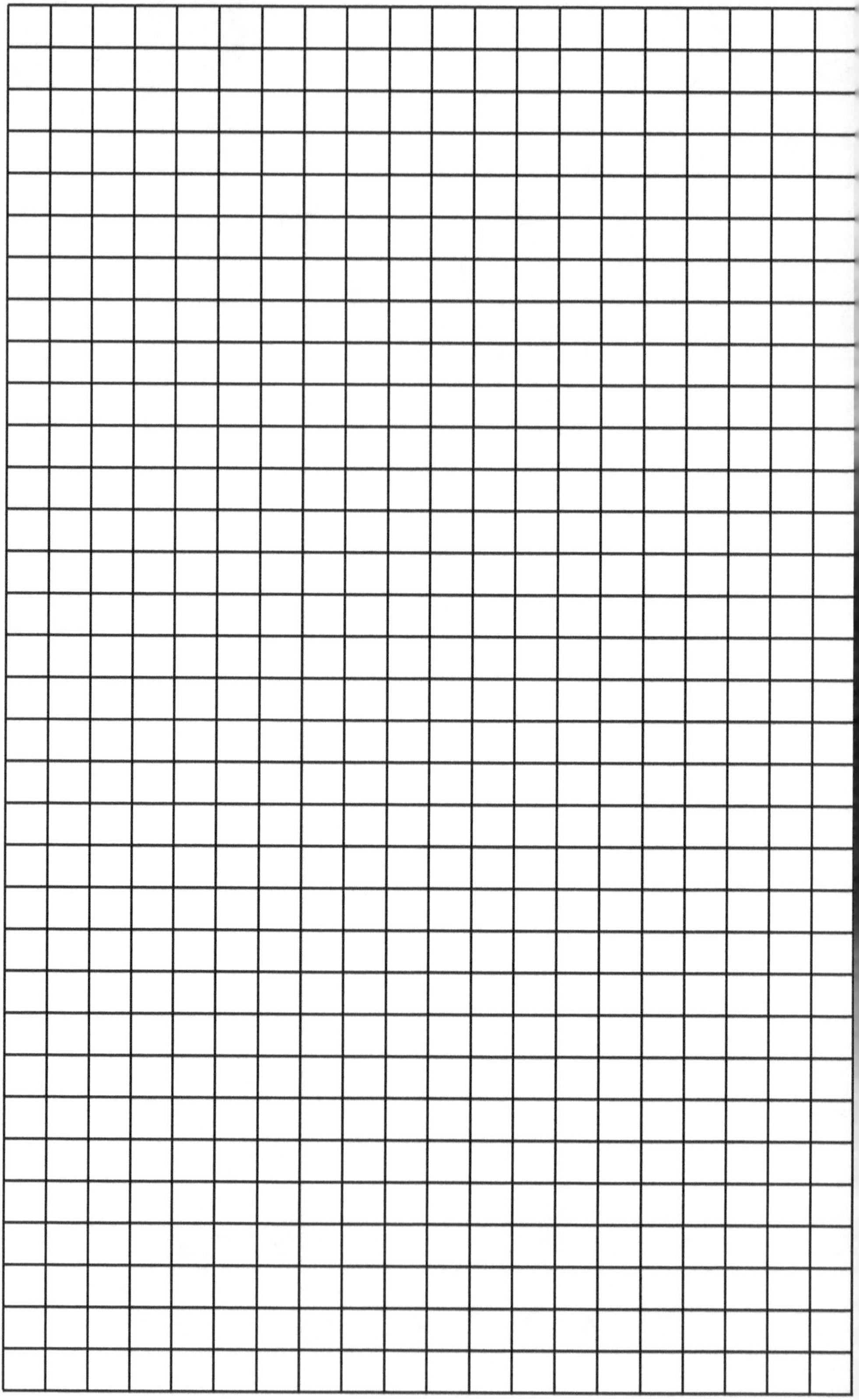

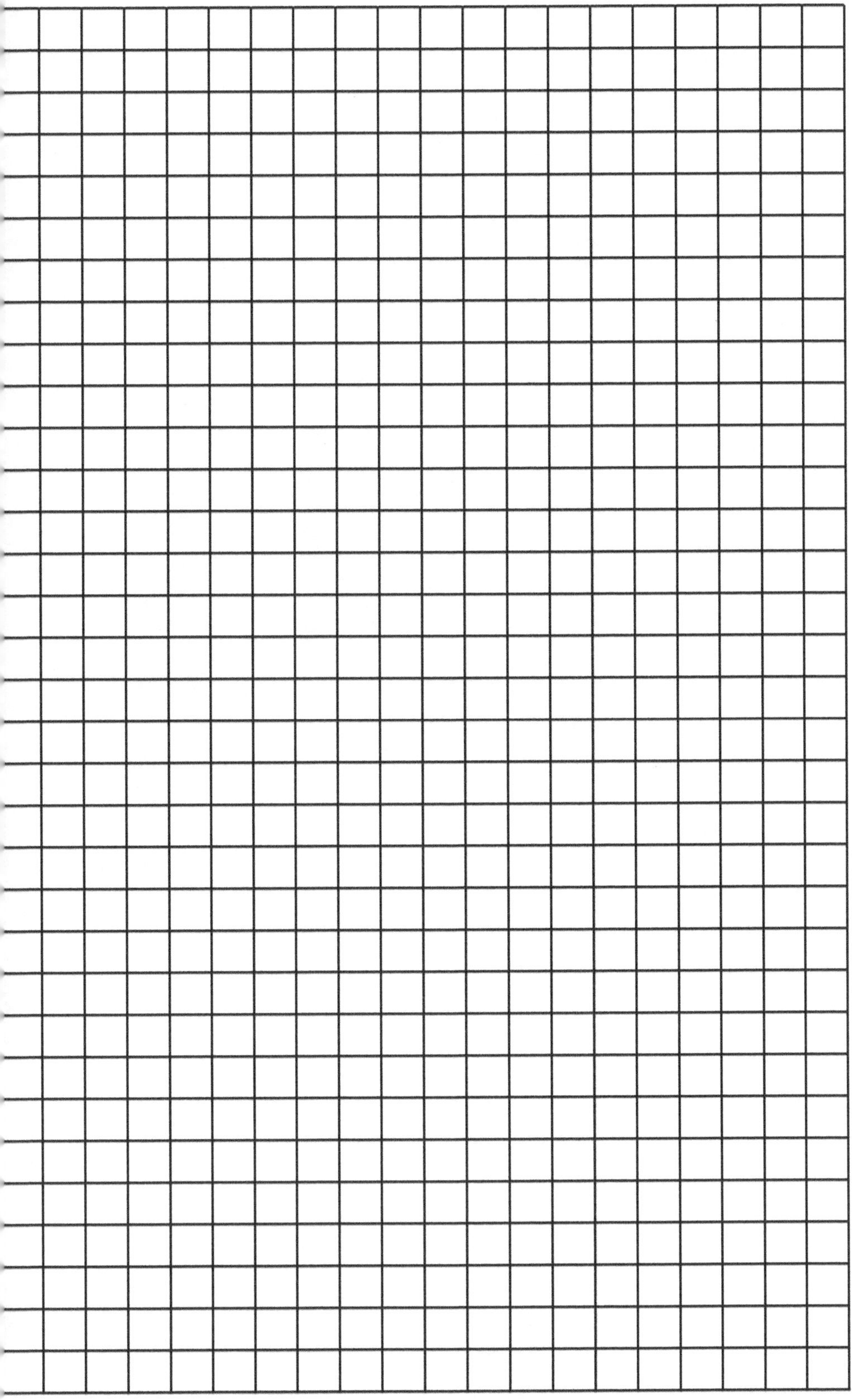

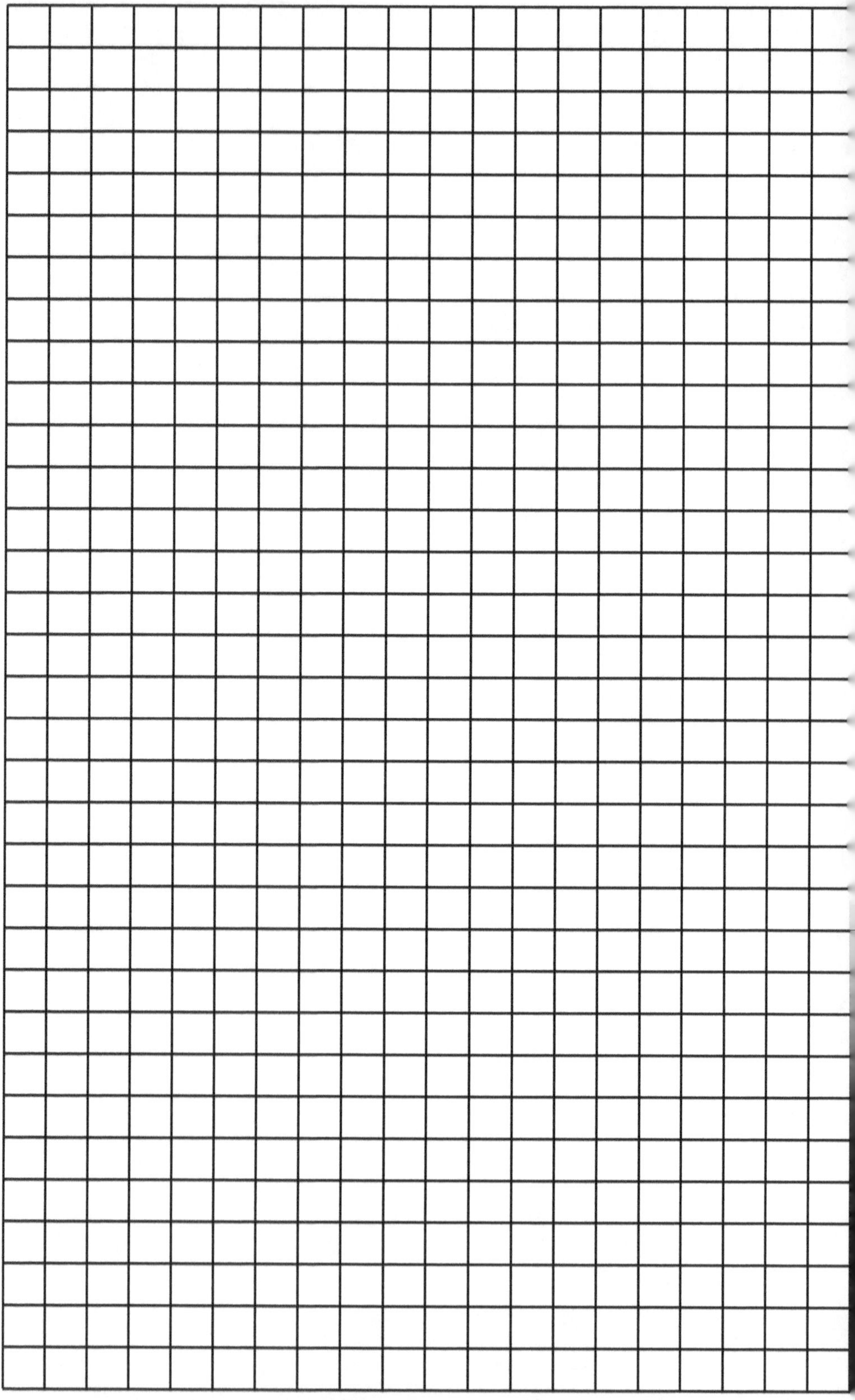

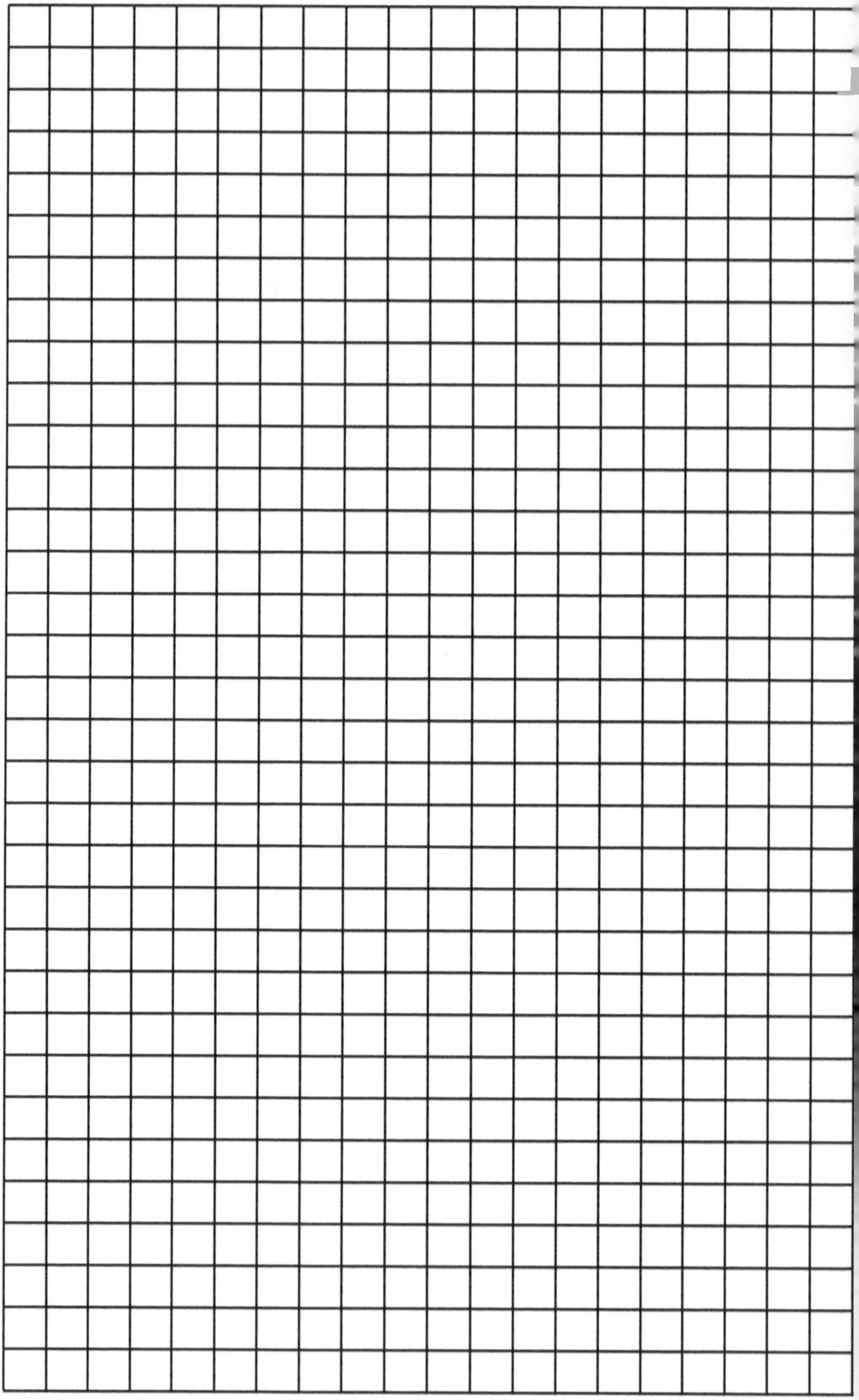

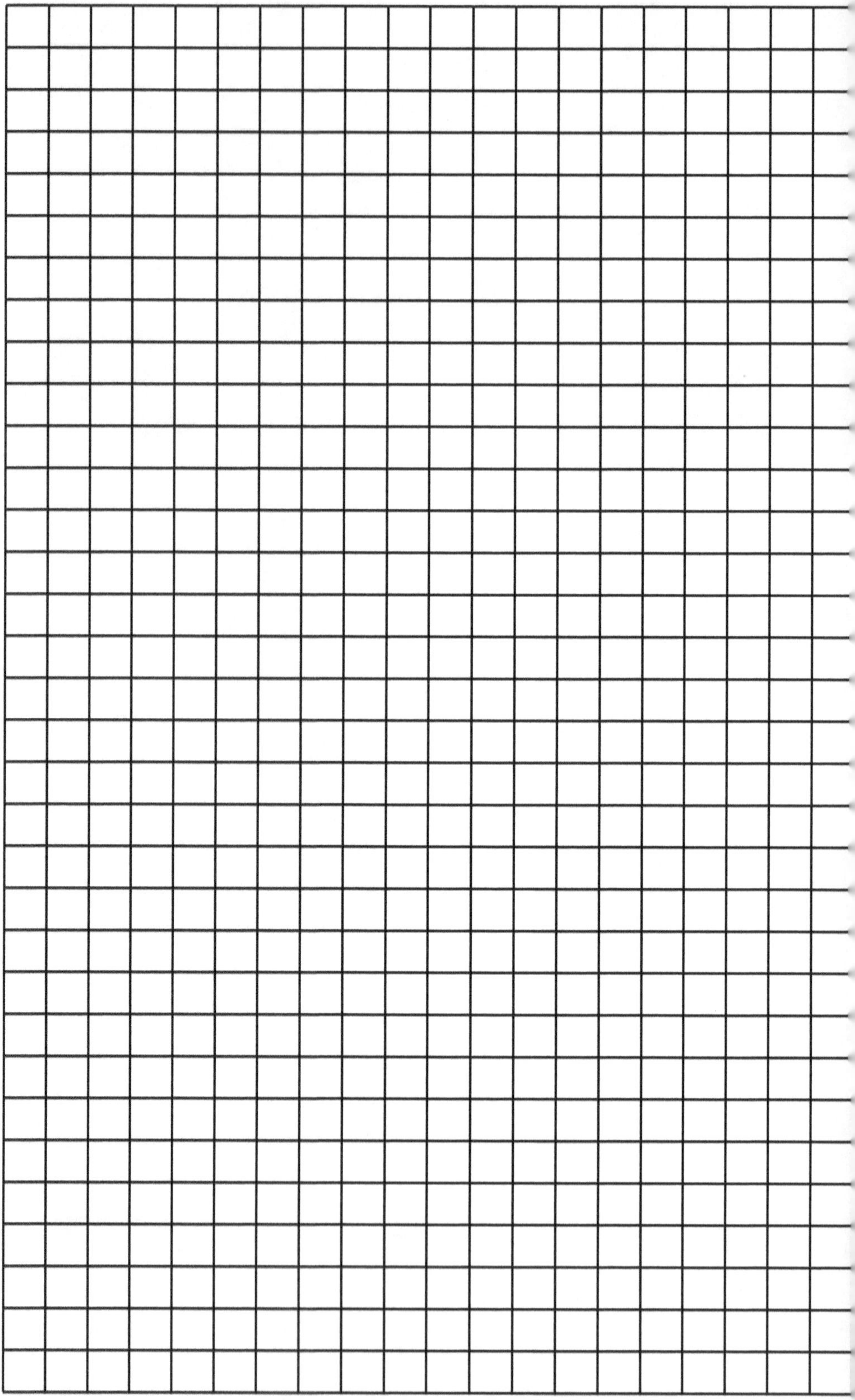

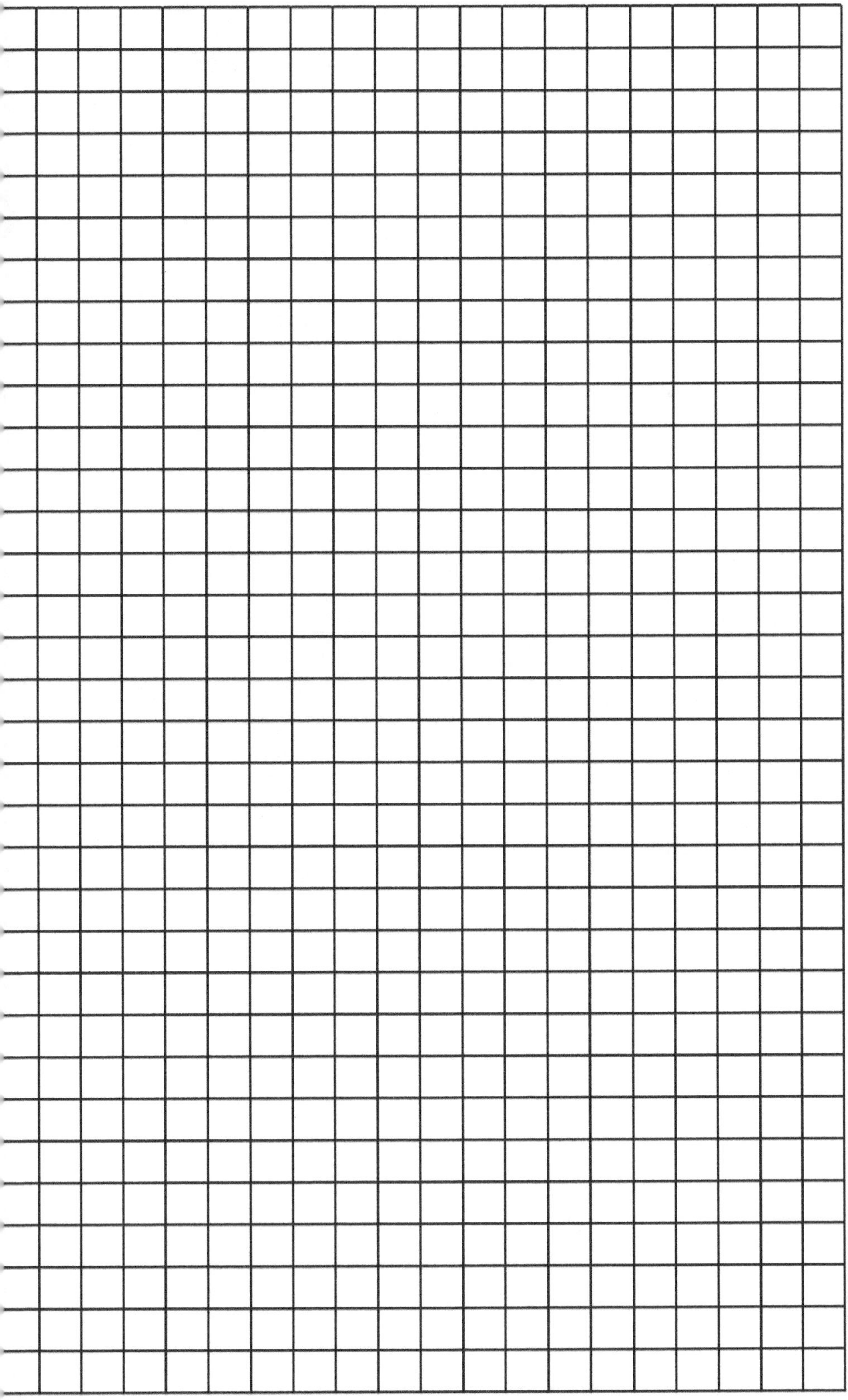

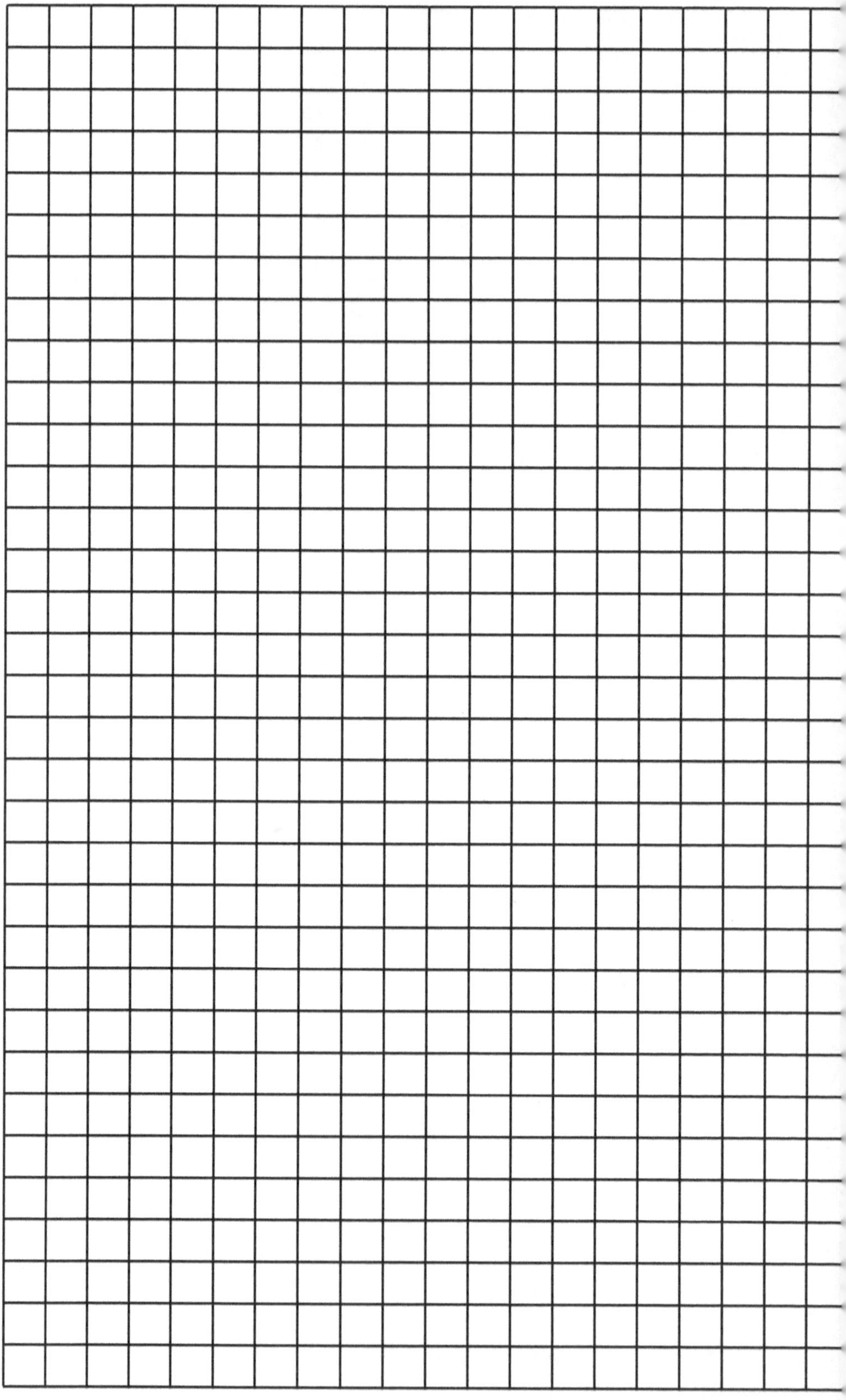

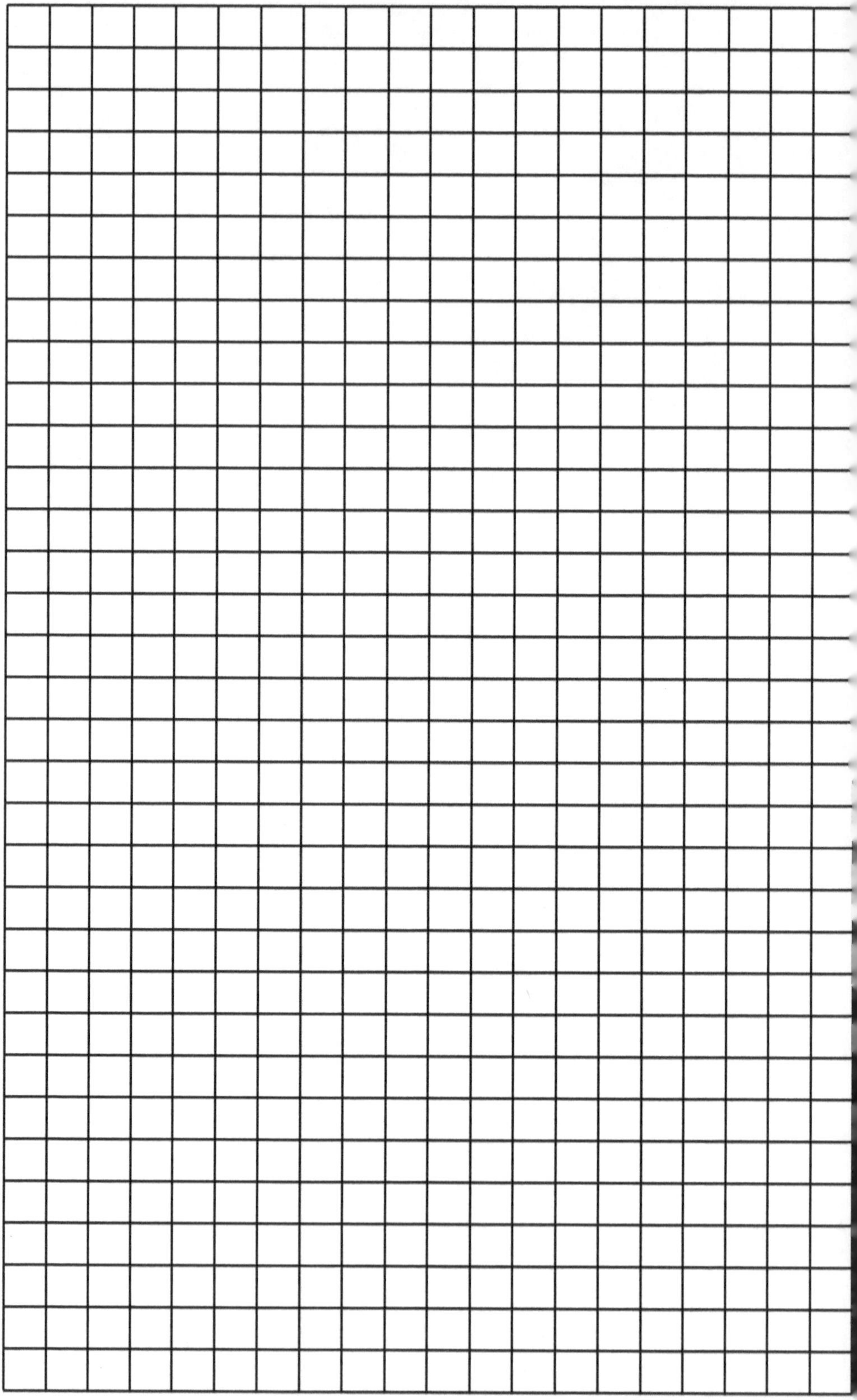

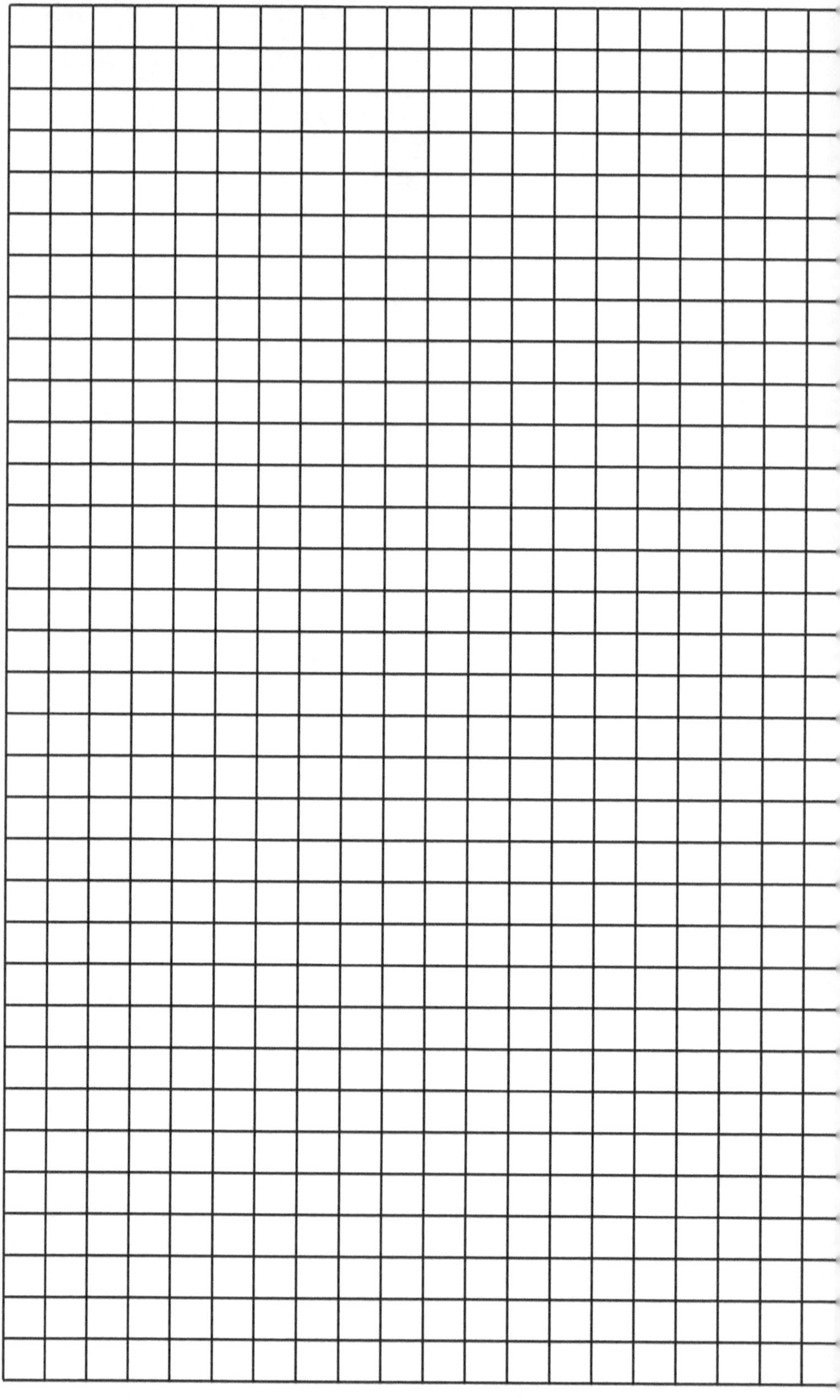

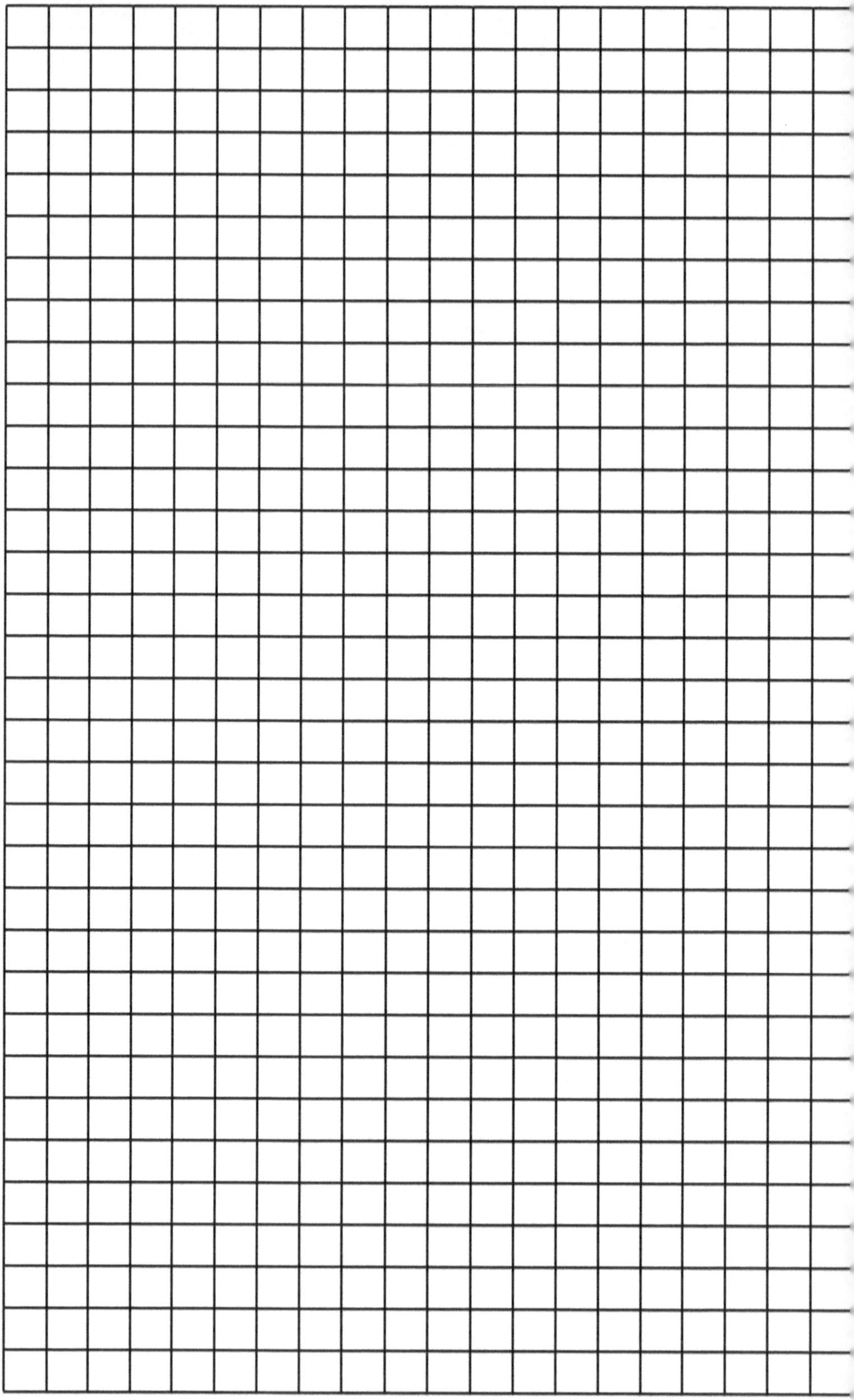

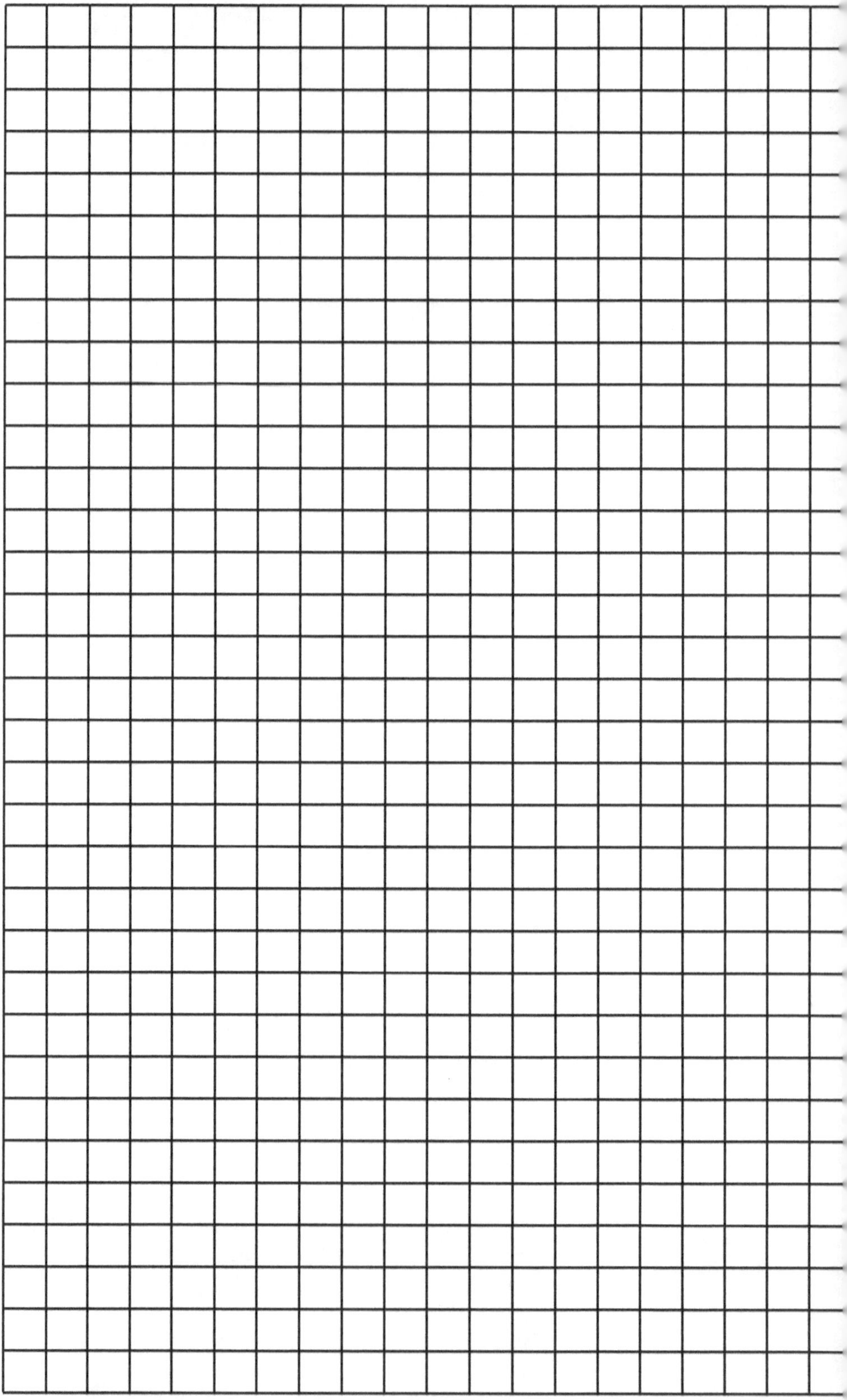

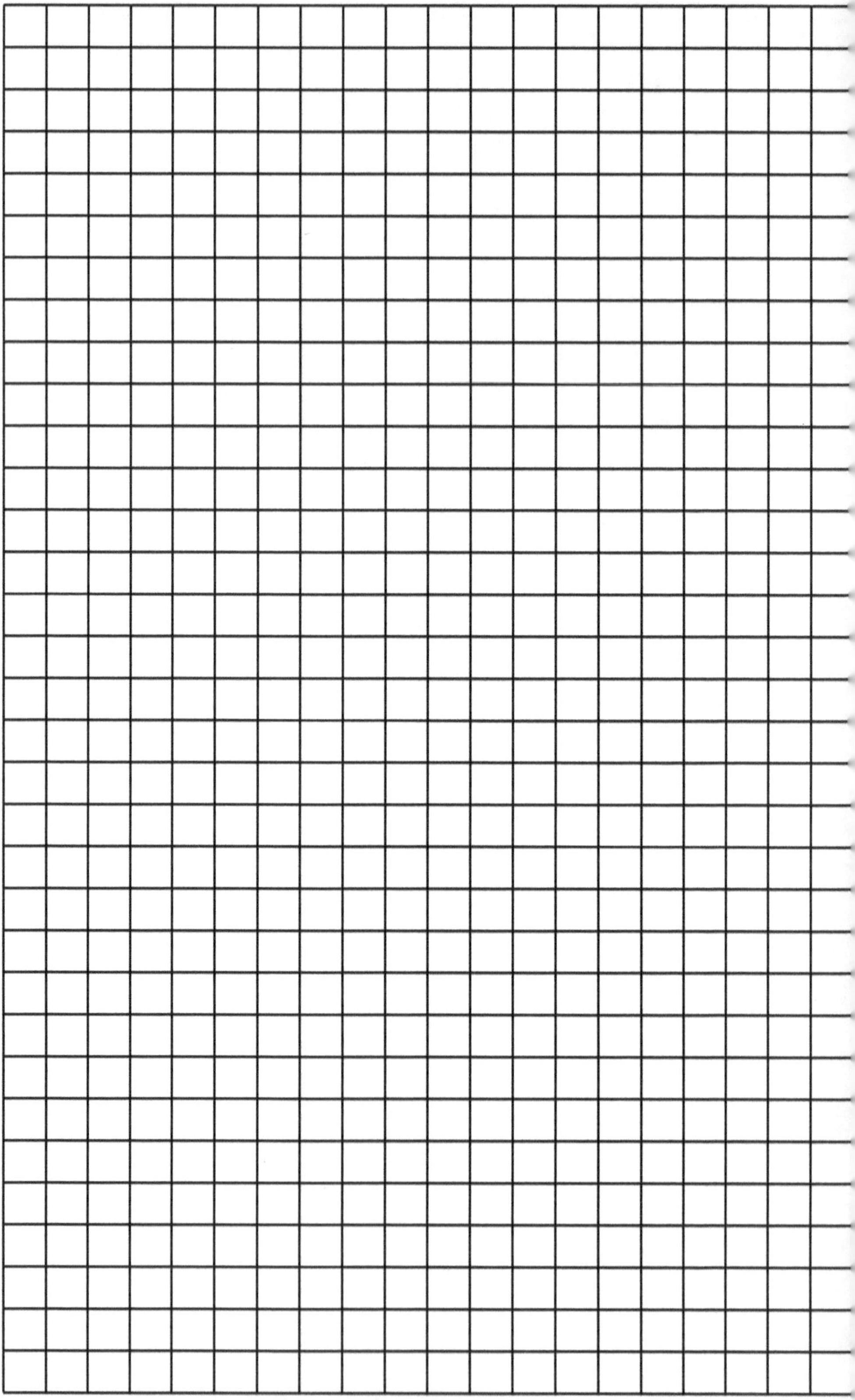

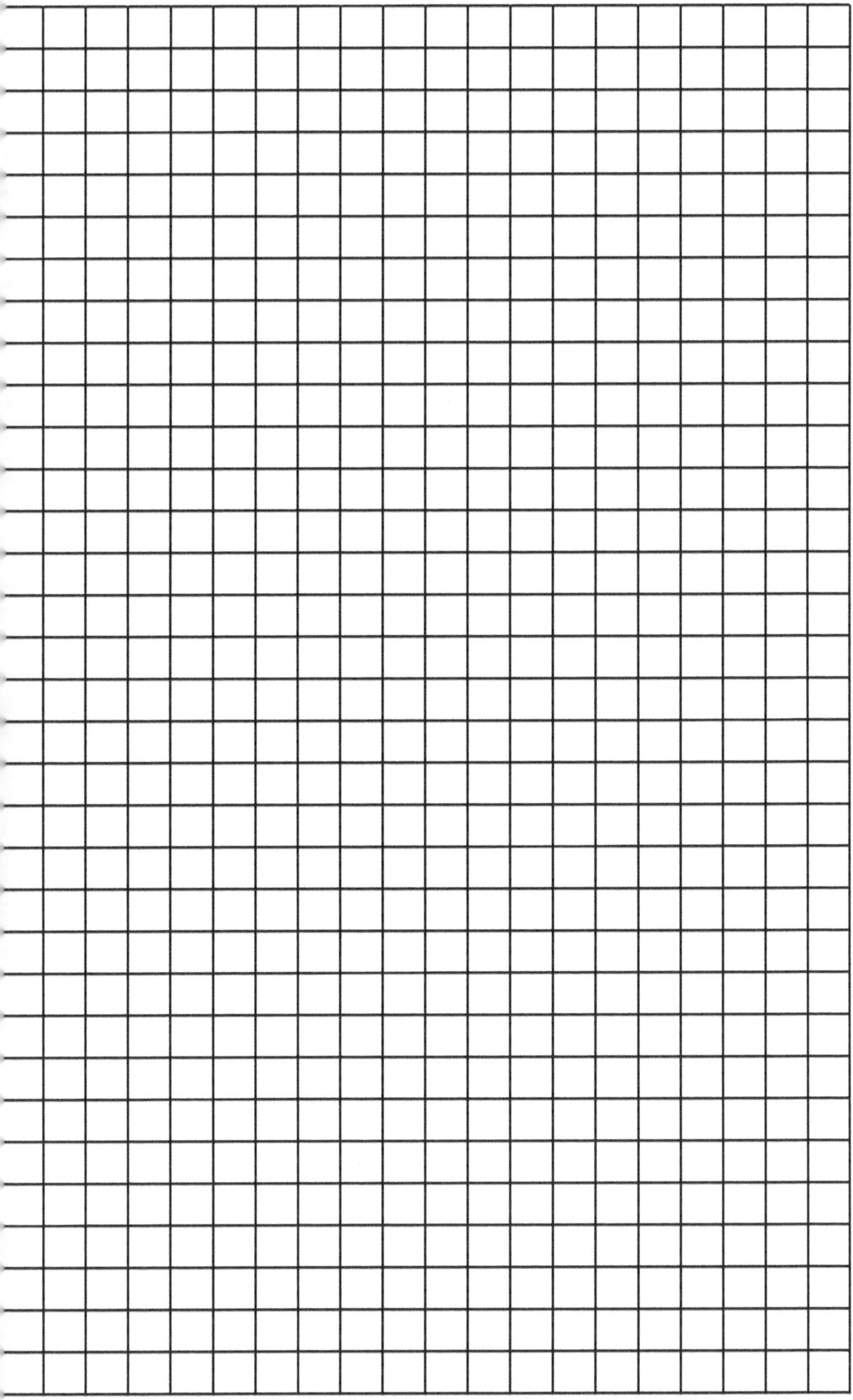

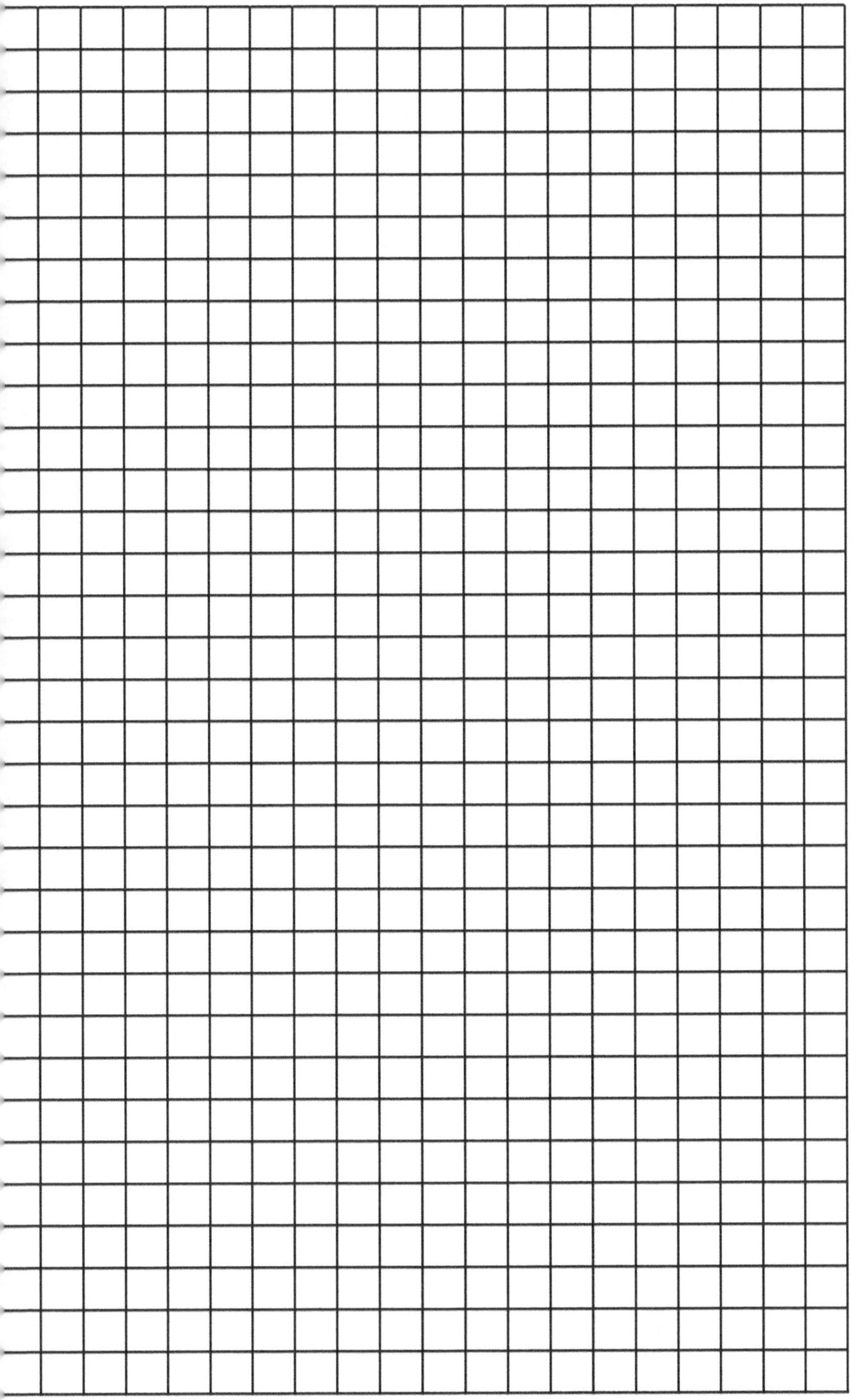

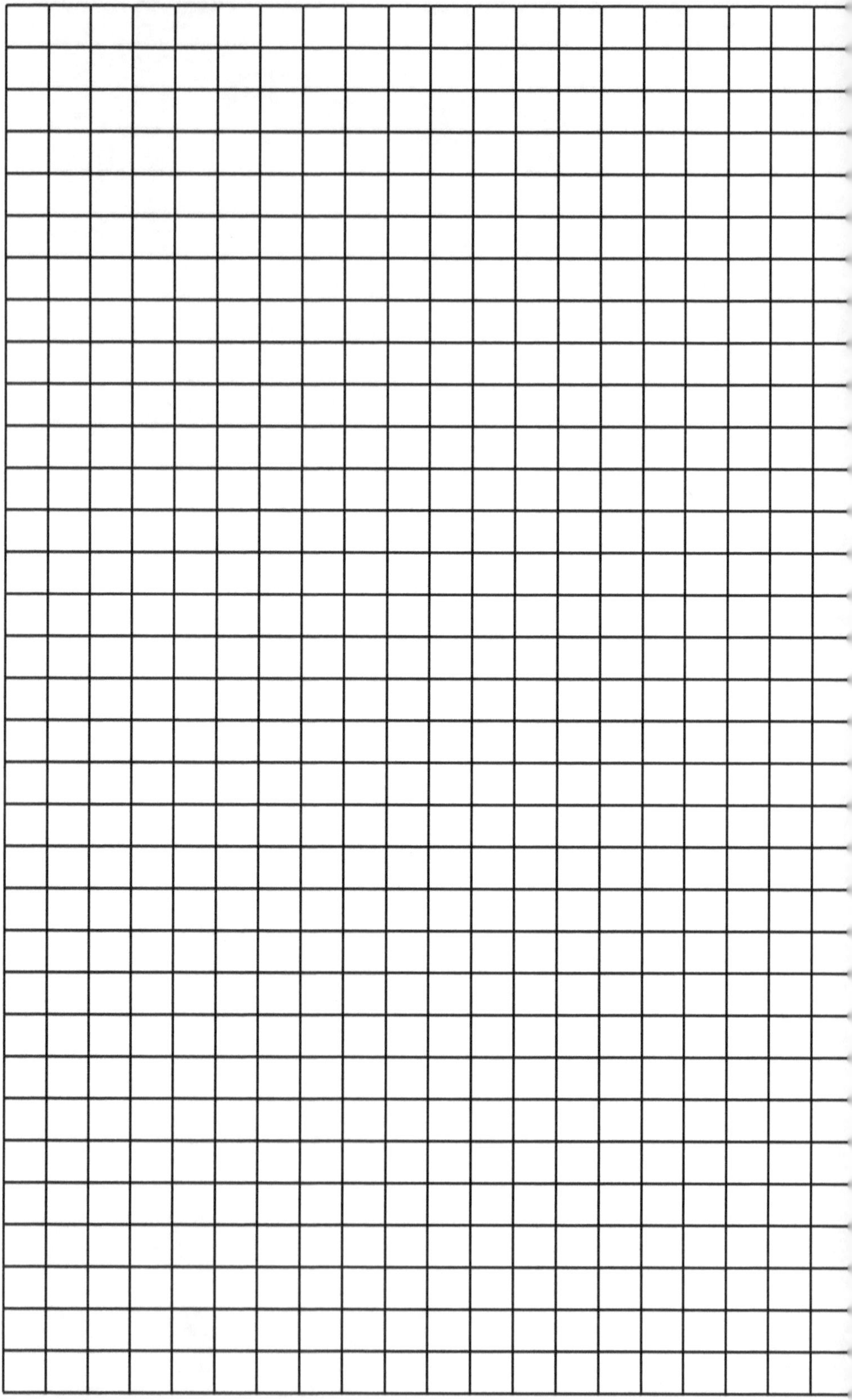

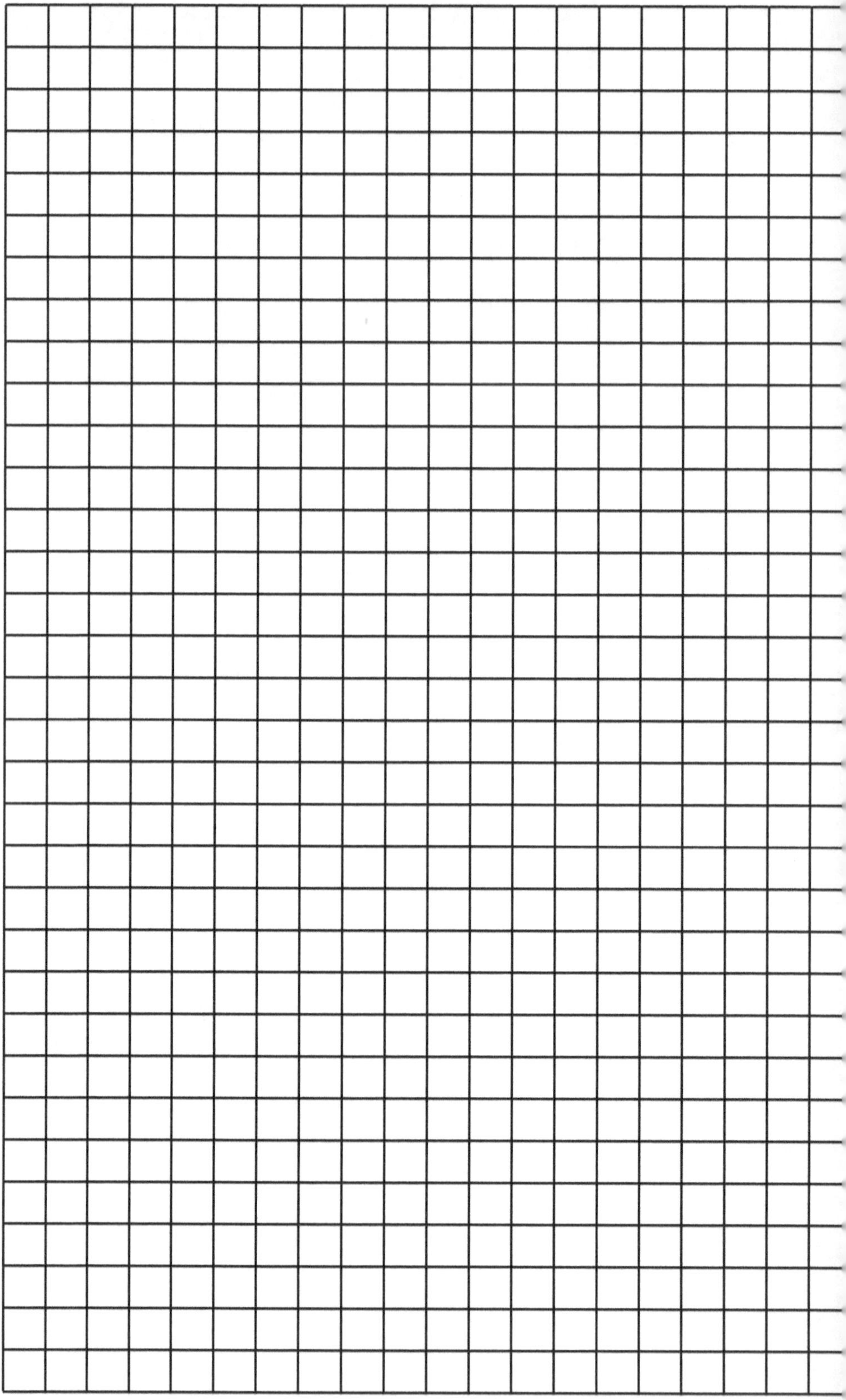

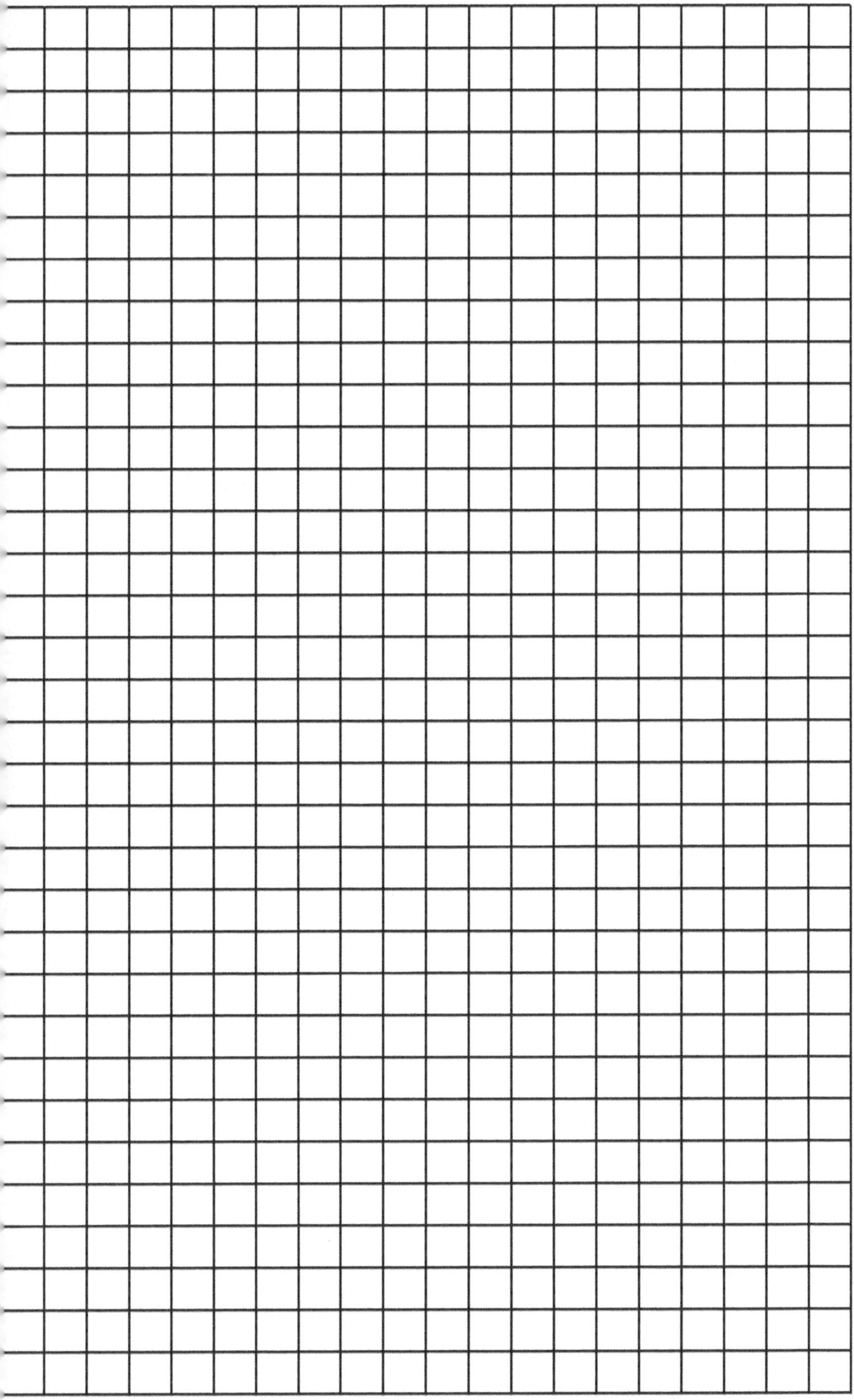

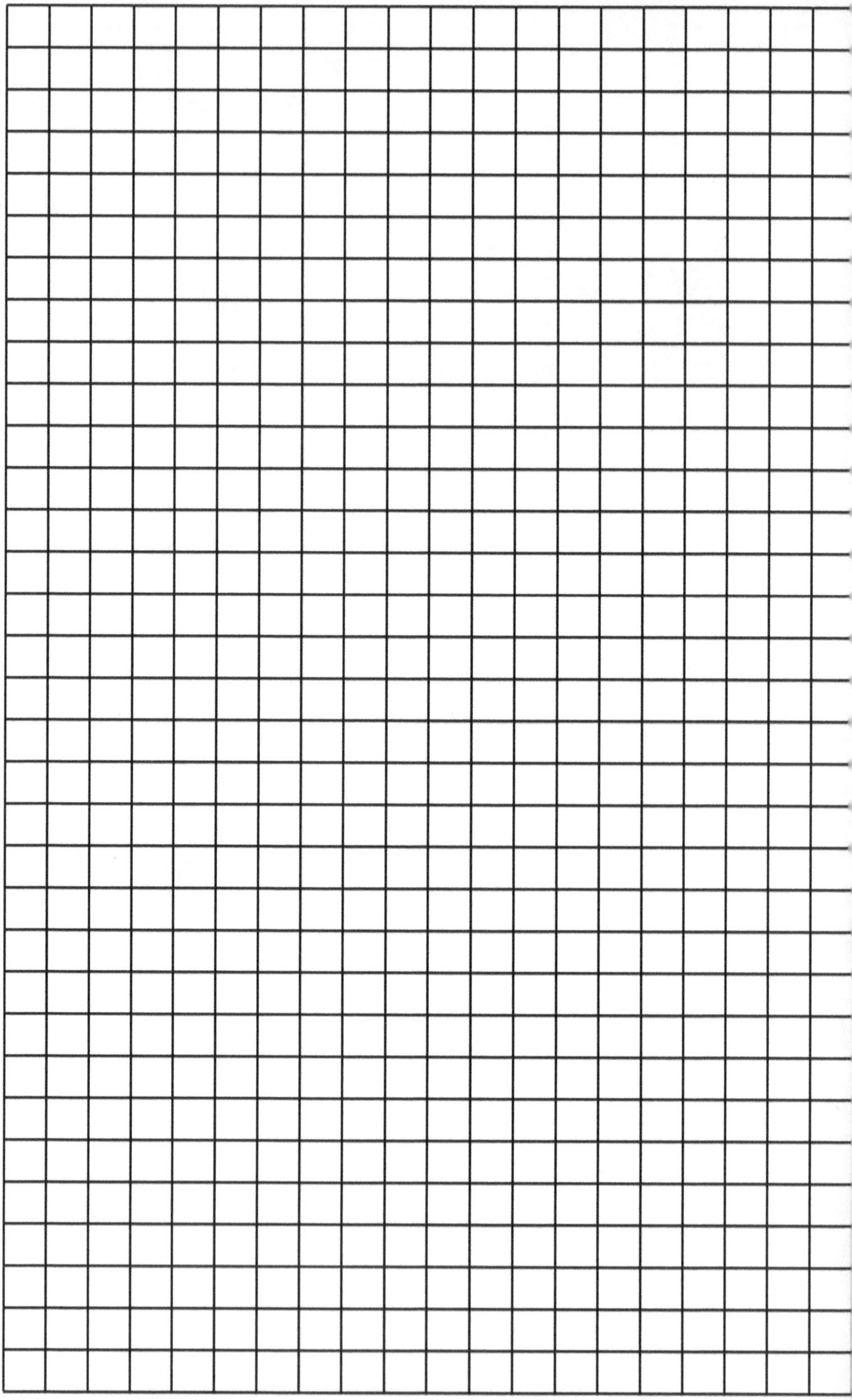

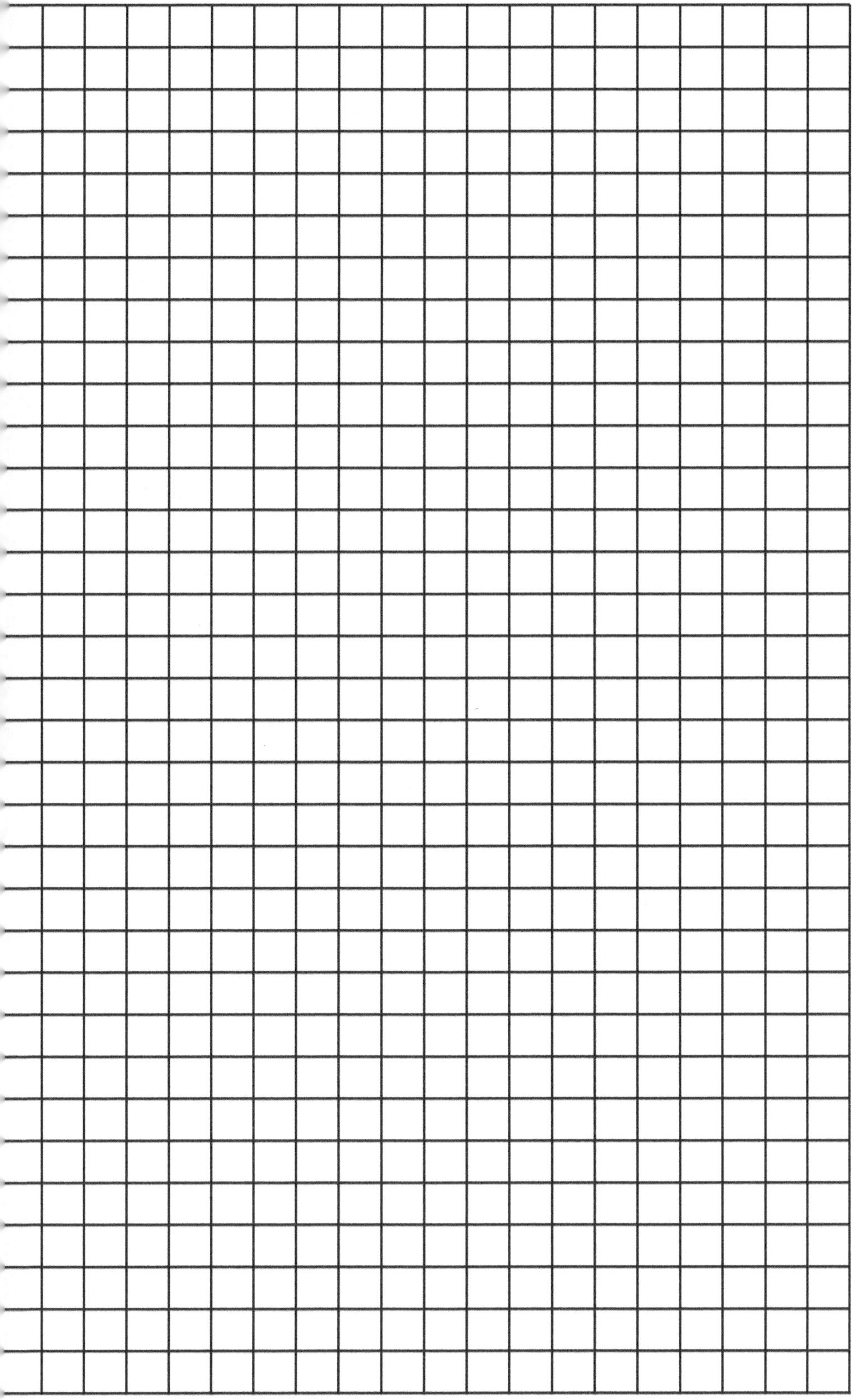

www.ingramcontent.com/pod-product-compliance
Lightning Source LLC
Chambersburg PA
CBHW030704220526
45463CB00005B/1904

* 9 7 8 1 6 5 2 6 8 7 6 5 8 *